CHEPO TEAM

A once local superhero team that consists of three brothers has been called many things by the mainstream media: vigilantes, racists, white supremacists. But for all the name calling they have received from enemies of the People, this team prefers to go by the Spanish slang for "great" and "awesome": CHEPO.

Their last adventure saw them going on a mission into space and take down Disney's Death Star which threatened to destroy the whole planet by turning everyone into homosexuals with its "Ray of Gay." But with a presidential election stolen from President Donald J. Trump and a mysterious virus that's turning people into crazies on the rise, the job seems to not be done.

WRITER:
JUAN PABLO VILLACIS

ART/COLORS/LETTERS:
JUAN PABLO VILLACIS

COVERS:
JUAN PABLO VILLACIS

CHEPO TEAM CREATED BY
JUAN PABLO VILLACIS

ORLANDO VANS: SUPERHERO. TWIN BROTHER. CHEPO TEAM'S MOST SELF-DISCIPLINED MEMBER.

BERNARDO VANS: SUPERHERO. TWIN BROTHER. CHEPO TEAM'S REBELLIOUS MEMBER.

J.P. VANS: SUPERHERO. BROTHER. CHEPO TEAM'S NAIVE BUT BRAVE CAPTAIN.

PAPI: CHEPO TEAM'S FATHER. THE MOST POLITICALLY INCORRECT DAD IN COMIC BOOK HISTORY.

BRAD VANS: CHEPO TEAM'S BROTHER. TOUGH AND TALENTED ATHLETE. CAN BE RUDE SOMETIMES.

LA NINA: CHEPO TEAM'S SISTER AND YOUNGEST OF THE FAMILY. DAD'S FAVORITE CHILD. A BIT OF A WORRIER.

LA SOMBRA: SUPERVILLAIN. FORMER RULER OF AMERICA AND EUROPE. REVENGE IS HIS FUEL.

RAPTOR: SUPERVILLAIN. FORMER RULER OF AFRICA. UNREASONABLE PREDATOR WHO LOVES CHAOS.

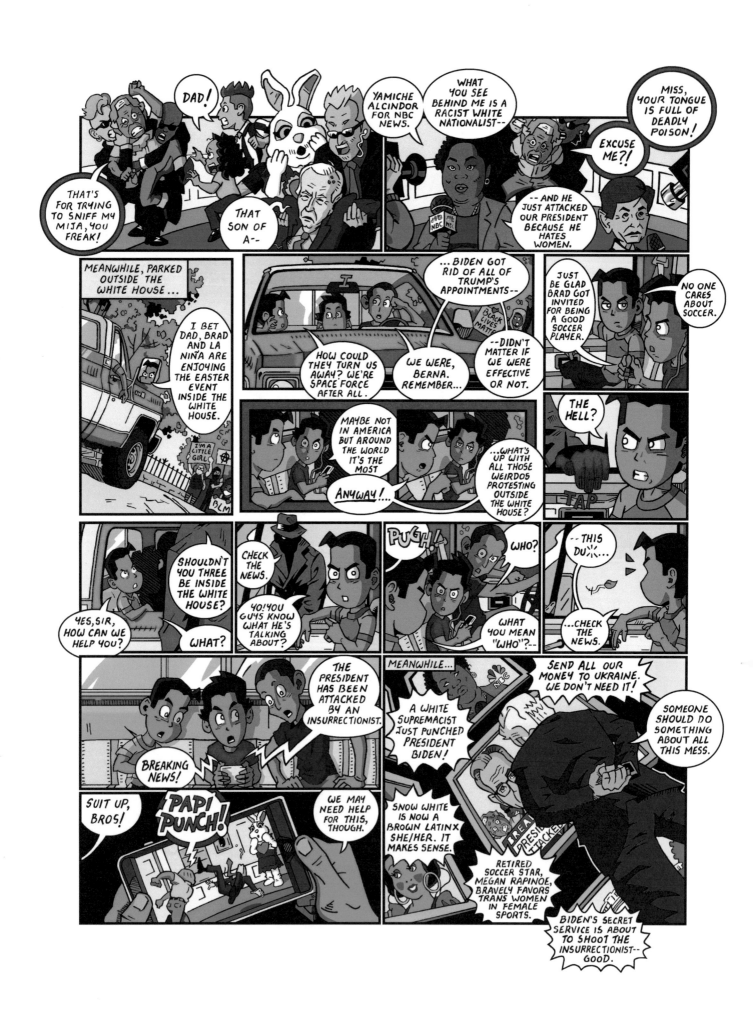

To Be Continued...

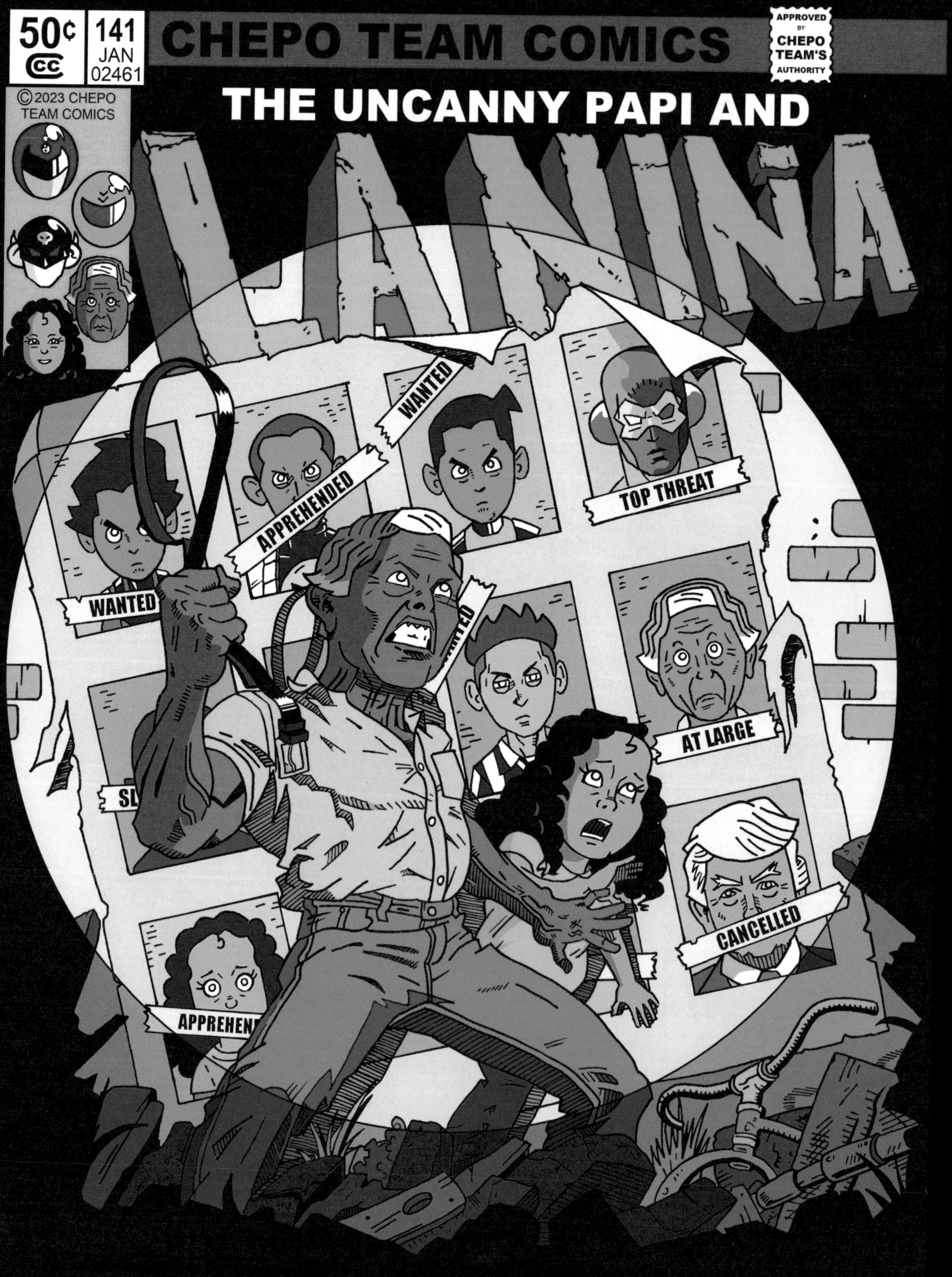
50¢
CC
141
JAN
02461
CHEPO TEAM COMICS
APPROVED BY CHEPO TEAM'S AUTHORITY
©2023 CHEPO TEAM COMICS
THE UNCANNY PAPI AND
LA NIÑA
WANTED
APPREHENDED
WANTED
TOP THREAT
WANTED
AT LARGE
CANCELLED

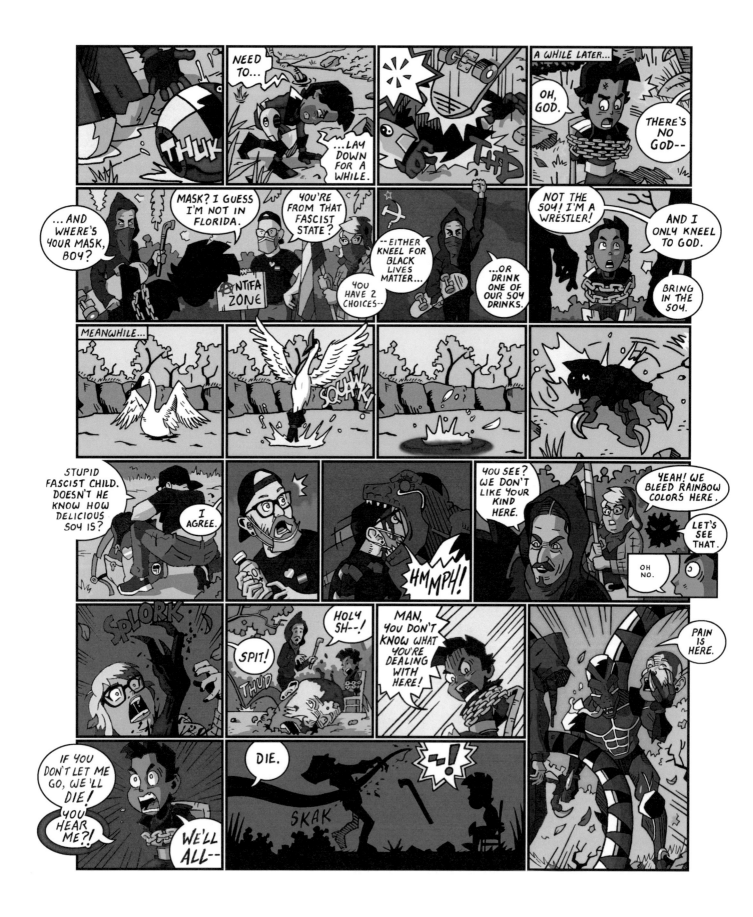

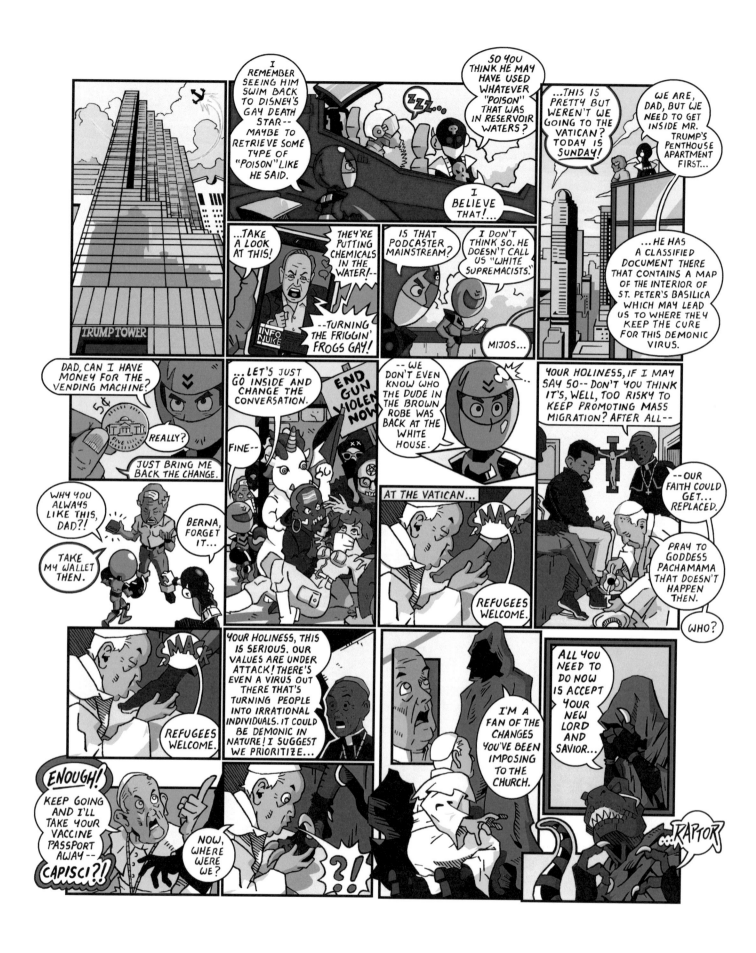

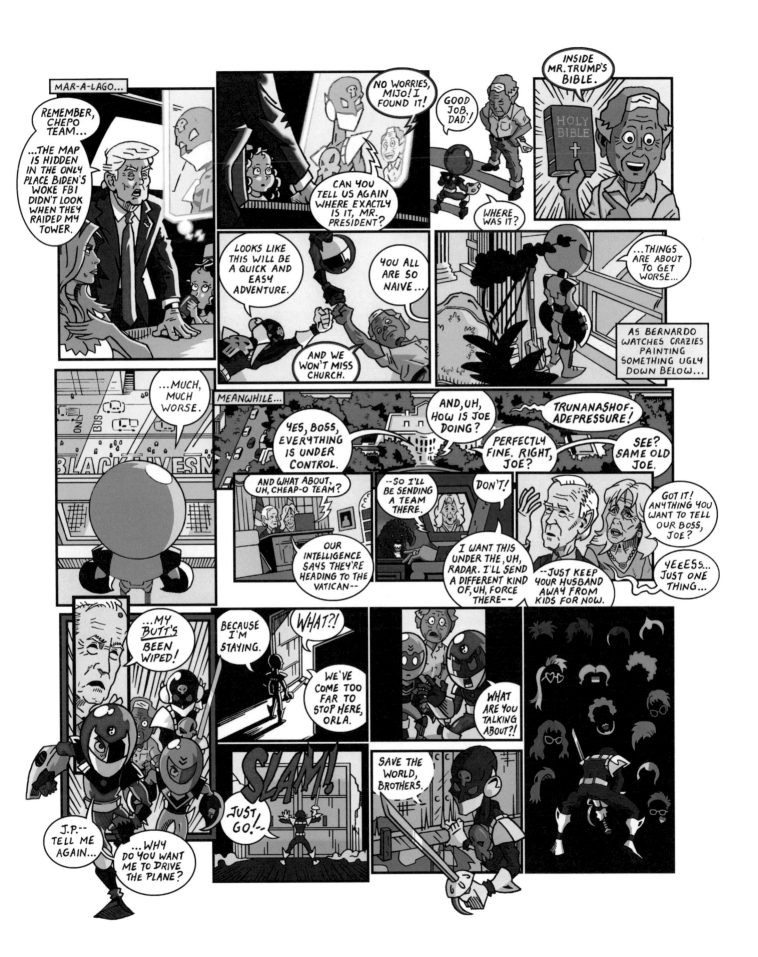

To Be Concluded...

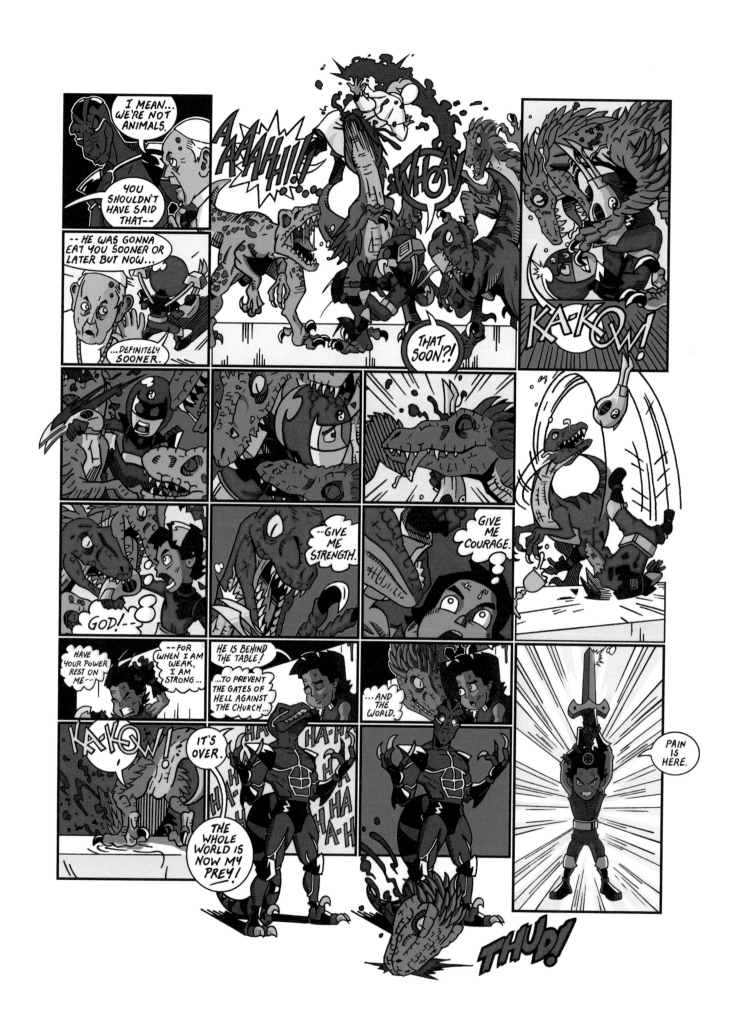

THE END?

Made in the USA
Columbia, SC
29 October 2024

44726711R00020